Black Bears

Titans of the Forest

Dr. Richard A. NeSmith

Love of Nature Series

ISSUE 10

Applied Principles of Education & Learning

APE-Learning

FLESCH-KINCAID GRADE LEVEL: 7.3

Black Bear
(Ursus *americanus*)

The black bear is the most familiar and smallest of bears living in North America. The very first thing to learn about American black bears is that they are not all black. They come in a variety of colors besides black, including brown, cinnamon, and even extremely rare blue-gray, blue-black, and white. However, their features are very different from other bears in America, such as the brown bears (including the grizzly) and polar bears.

Range

Historically, the black bear lives in most of North America, including Alaska, Canada, and most of the lower 48 United States, and Mexico. The black bear population in North America, excluding cubs, is estimated to be from 600,000 to 700,000. About 55% live in Canada. Another 40% live in the United States. The 5% left live in Mexico, where their territory is significantly reduced. In the continental United States, they live in less than 20% of their *original* range. They are considered a stable species, and in some areas (California), their populations have increased due to conservation efforts.

Characteristics

Black bears can grow to be 4 to 7 feet tall when standing, and 3 feet high when standing on all four feet. They weigh from 200 to as much as 600 pounds. Size correlates with both age and region. Black bears have some essential distinctions that enable one to identify them in comparison

with brown bears and polar bears. Black bears have a straight face and flat shoulders. It has ears that are generally pointed and has a short tail. Black bears, and their young cubs, are agile climbers. They are also at home in the water and are efficient runners, reaching speeds of up to 30 miles an hour (48.3 kph).

Black bears are very adaptable. They are quite intelligent and curious. They are much shyer than the other bear species and generally avoid confrontations. We will see that records of personal attacks are scarce.

Diet

In some ways, a black bear will eat anything that doesn't eat them. And, almost nothing eats them. It is all about calories for bears, so they will eat it if they can find it. They are at the top of the food chain. Black bears are

opportunistic but not picky eaters. They generally look for the meal that requires the least amount of energy or struggle to obtain. They are omnivores, and they will eat field grasses, roots, tubers, nuts, berries of all kinds, fruits, and other foods. They also eat ants, grubs, termites, beetles, and other insects. They will eat *carrion* (dead animals). Black bears like salmon and different kinds of fish and will hunt for small mammals, including small pets, if available where they venture. It is not uncommon for black bears to feast on deer fawns (when they can catch them). They will also hunt for rabbit nests and baby birds. The average black bear diet usually is 80 percent vegetable, 15 percent insect, and 5 percent small animals, reptiles, and eggs.

Unfortunately, they also quickly develop a fondness for human foods and garbage. This is bad for their health, and bears become dangerous when they get **habituated** (accustomed to) obtaining food from humans. People are not seen as a food item. Still, their willingness to tolerate people and the proximity that bears will be

comfortable with humans is not safe. Humans must be particularly careful with storing food at campsites, cabins, or rural homes. It is never a good idea to feed bears, but it is also illegal in many states. Missouri wildlife biologist, Josh Wisdom, shared that eventually, "a fed bear is a dead bear."

The problem is complex, for most people do not intentionally feed bears. Ninety percent of the time, people aren't putting food out for bears. But they are putting birdseed out for birds, and bears are eating it. "In their mind, it's not feeding the bears because that's not donuts, and they don't put it out for bears" (Josh Wisdom). But the

bear still comes every day and eats there, creating the same problem as if they were handing out donuts. Some communities with a large bear presence have asked or made an ordinance that bird feeders are not permitted. Other communities have "bear watches," in which residents are notified of a bear sighting. They then remove their bird feeders.

American black bears, being one of the largest animals in the forest, are almost always hungry. They must consume about 90 to 100 pounds of food per day. They are "eating machines," but for a good reason. Also, we will see that is a lot of poop!

Black bears spend their winter season in the form of
hibernation (dormant) in their dens. It is noted, however,

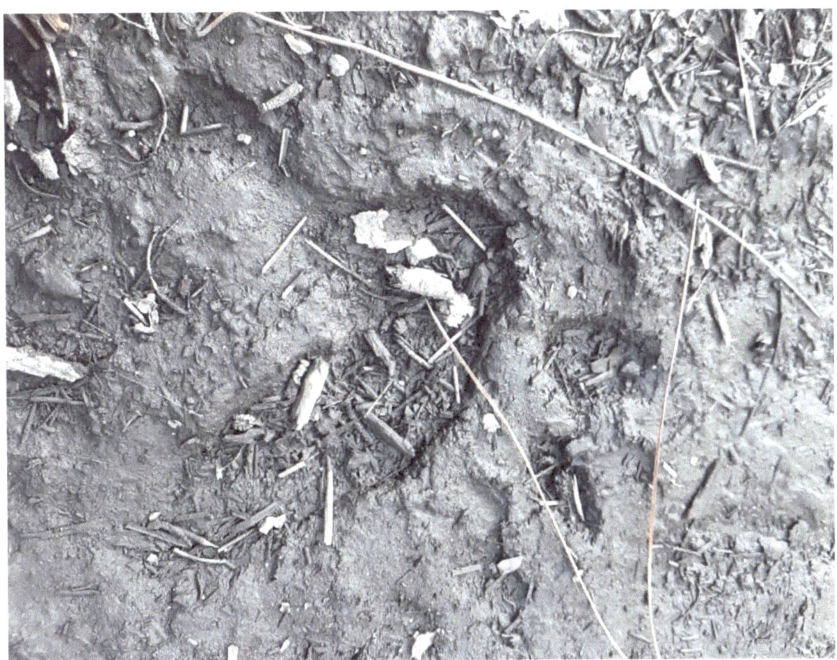

that this is not true hibernation; instead, it is a form of
denning. This state, also called ursid hibernation or carnivore
lethargy, is a form of **torpor**. Before this "rest" period
occurs, they eat ravenously in summer and autumn to build
up and bulk up the needed fat. Bears consume 5,000
calories per day, but by autumn, that count jumps to 20,000
calories per day! That's a 400% increase in food! This
period of feeding frenzy is called *hyperphagia.* This passion
for food is the reason why birdseed and human food are so
attractive, so calorie-rich compared to eating acorns.

This tiredness that results from hibernation is a period brought on by three factors:

1. low activity
2. followed by intermittent light sleep while
3. experiencing a slower metabolism.

Also, lethargy is induced by reproductive status, food availability, amount of daylight, and temperature change. For example, urban bears in some towns do not hibernate at all if they are regular trash bears. A bear that can eat all winter will not hibernate. Hibernation is a way of solving the natural problem of not having enough food in the winter.

The temperature has a critical role in the length of sleep. In warmer southern states, bears den for shorter periods and sleep less deeply than bears in colder climates. Bears in northern states are much more sluggish and less responsive to people than bears in the South who readily run away when people have come near their dens. In even warmer states, such as Florida, male bears may have a reduced denning period or none at all. The reason is that warmer climates have more food available for more extended

periods, sometimes to the point that hibernation doesn't occur at all.

During the hibernation period, they are continually feeding on body fat during these long sleep periods. Even during hibernation, it is not uncommon for the bear to exit the den and bring in fresh leaves or to sun. For example, bears in Missouri might enter the den in November but might leave around Christmas and bring in more leaves. Or they might go just outside the den to sit in the sun on a warm day in January. They reenter the den and may not exit again until the end of March. Upon reawakening, they have only one thing on their minds, and that is to eat, even at the expense of going days with little or no sleep.

During hibernation, bears recycle their urine to prevent dehydration. Also, their muscles do not atrophy. This normal physical response is a natural response of muscles not used for some time. It usually means loss of mass, protein, and strength. This muscle maintenance has caught space scientists' attention to help those who would be traveling in space. Research is being looked at to get astronauts' muscles to do what bear muscles experience in hibernation. Upon awakening, a bear has to pass a fecal plug first, so it begins eating green vegetation to start the stomach to working again.

Most bears, including black bears, have almost super strength and can grip their prey with very sharp teeth and claws. In some states, it has been noted that bears will attack other predators to scavenge their prey. So much so that wolves are on the lookout for bears who often monitor their hunting activities. And, bears can be ferocious when threatened or when defending their cubs.

The worst place to be in the entire world is between a mother bear and her cubs. However, almost always, a black bear will run away or run the cubs up a tree, following suit pretty quickly.

Habitat

Black bears prefer lots of foliage. They typically live in forests but are also found in mountains and swamps. But they also like a variety of food sources from which to choose. Both factors vitally important when raising their cubs. But they are highly adaptive to many different habitats.

Bears also live in large urban areas like that found in New Jersey, which has the densest population of bears in the nation. Or, municipal Asheville, North Carolina, where they have a vast urban bear project there. *Black bears are big raccoons and live anywhere that you can have coons.*[1] Home includes fence rows in agricultural country, wilderness, and in towns. They might prefer a large expanse of forest, but they don't have to have it.

Bears often make a den under a rock ledge, under a fallen tree, in a hollow tree, or a brush pile from logging. Many dens are just holes in the ground under a root wad or dug into the side of a hill. Bears collect grass and leaves with which to pad their beds. Black bears also use "open dens," which is a bird's nest of leaves with no cover on it at all. After hibernation, which occurs following snowmelt and spring, they rarely sleep at all for the next two months, continually foraging. These dens, burrows, or caves provide a place to call home and give them security during the

---

[1] Josh Wisdom, Missouri Wildlife Biologist.

winter hibernation.

Behavior

Black bears males (boars), and females (sows) are solitary animals but can be found together during mating seasons. They roam vast territories, though they *share* them with other bears. Males tend to wander a 15- to 80-square-mile (38.5-208 square km) home range. This range varies significantly from one state to the next. There are urban bears on the East Coast with 5-mile home ranges and bears in Missouri with 100-mile ranges.

Bears have good senses. Do not think that they have poor eyesight. In fact, their vision is at least as good as the average human's. Bears have excellent night vision because of a reflective membrane on the back of their eye called the *tapetum lucidum*. Again, black bears have an acute hearing about twice as sensitive as humans and over a broader frequency range.

In almost all cases, black bears will hear the person approaching long before they can ever be spotted. Because of this, black bears will often move away before they are noticed.

The black bear's nose is even more remarkable. Without a doubt, *a bear's strongest sense is smell.* Bears have the most acute sense of smell of any other animal on earth. A bear's sense of smell is so sensitive that it can detect animal carcasses upwind and from a distance of 20 miles away.

Hikers should just assume that the black bear can smell the food in their food bag, too.

"A bear can smell the scent of a human in a footprint, ripe berries in the air, and a steak grilling a mile away." Wildlife biologists have found that bears can *smell seven times better than a bloodhound*, the dogs most used for tracking lost people. Its big nose has an area inside (called the *nasal mucosa*) 100 times larger than ours. Bears are well equipped for survival in any forest or urban community. Indeed, a bear has a drug addict-like personality for *easy* food. One wildlife biologist put it this way: A bear is basically just a way that a stomach has found to move and fill itself!

Black bears make dens in caves, burrows, brush piles, or even in holes in large trees. Black bears den for various lengths of time. Denning is governed by the diverse climates in which they live. Female bears that are pregnant always enter the den first. Even a month ahead of the male bear. Often hunting seasons are timed this way to prevent the shooting of females.

Black bears are inquisitive animals. This snooping, along  with a passion for food, often leads to campground tents or RV's being raided. They do a lot of sniffing and may stand up on hind legs to better view and smell their surroundings. This posture is normal behavior and not a sign of aggression.

Bears respond to humans just as they would other bears. Understanding how a bear responds is essential in coexisting with them. The first thing is to understand that bears are comparatively quiet creatures. They only make noises when seeking to communicate. For example, cubs cry and moan when upset. They grunt or make a purring sound when wanting to suckle[2] (drink their mother's milk). Females communicate with their young by grunting or moaning to let the cubs know to head up a tree for safety

---

[2] Josh Wisdom shared regarding cubs suckling, "it sounds like a machine gun."

or to have them follow her.

Both male and female black bears and bears of all ages mark trees with their scent. Black bears rub, bite and claw marks onto trees between 5 and 7 feet high. These marks often occur along defined animal trails. Trees, wooden sign-posts, and even utility poles are marked. However, most of the markings are done by mature males during the mating season (May and June in the North and June and July in the South).

Black bears frequently rub their shoulders, neck, head, or back up against the tree bark. They also will claw and bite the tree. The claw marks are usually shallow, yet incisor marks can be deep enough to cause the bark to stand out or be removed entirely. A bear will stand up and bite a tree, twisting its head and grinding with the upper and lower canine teeth on one side of its mouth. The bites look like dots and dashes caused by the upper and lower canine teeth coming together.

It appears that black bears prefer trees with little vegetation to restrict access. The marking of trees coincides with the time when bears are shedding their winter coat. The fur is easily caught between the bark. So, trees that have been marked often have hair caught in the bark 2 to 5 feet (0.6 – 1.5 meters) above the ground, while the bite marks are 5 ½ to 6 ½ feet (1.7 – 2 m) high. In due time, the hair will bleach or lose its color and appear brown or blond.

Some naturalists have suggested that when you enter a wooded area, check the utility poles if you want to know whether bears live nearby. For some unknown reason, the bite marks are lower on the poles than on the trees. We do not understand why bears are so fond of marking trees, but it seems very important to them. Exactly why this is so is uncertain. There are several ideas as to why this may be so.

❶ it is a demonstration of male dominance.
❷ it communicates breeding status to ensure a mate
❸ it serves to help orient bears in lesser-known territories
❹ it ensures home range boundaries include females

Whatever the reason, bears invest a great deal of their time marking trees. Trees often have older marks and scars, as

well as newer ones, indicating repeated use. So, next time you take a hike, pay attention to the trees. They are bear indicators.

Reproduction

Boars and sows bears have numerous mating partners in any given season. Sows give birth to two to six blind and helpless cubs in mid-winter and nurse them in the den

until springtime when all emerge in search of food. The bear sleuth (group or family of bears) leaves the den well-rested but extremely hungry. The cubs will stay with their very protective mother for 12 to 18 months.

Mating season varies depending on habitat climate, but breeding usually occurs from May through August. Pregnancy (gestation) lasts between 60-70 days. Cubs are generally born during the hibernation stage in January or early February. The cubs, each ranging from one-half to one pound (226-453 g), will get their mother's attention and will cuddle up next to her for suckling when not sleeping. While in the den, cubs, from birth, gain a pound a week (this is used by biologists to age them). The cubs may wake sporadically, but they will not leave the den until early spring when they are vibrant, ravished, and begin almost

tirelessly to feed. That first spring, they put on weight quickly.

The mother bear spends the next year weaning, feeding, and teaching her cubs what to eat, where to find food, what to avoid, and how to survive. After that 1 ½ year training period, the cubs venture out on their own to establish their own territory. The estimated survival rate of black bears is about 86% in Florida to 73% in Virginia and North

Carolina.

Sadly, the fact is that many black bear cubs are more at risk than adult bears and do not reach adulthood due to hunting and attacks from predators. The female is unable to get pregnant until she is 3-5 years old. She will generally mate every two years, but this depends significantly on food supply, age, environment, and habitat density. The mortality rate for younger black bear cubs is about 15 to 35%. Typically, a sow's first litter does not survive because she lacks parenting experience. After losing her first litter, she improves as a mother and then produces cubs every other year for up to 20 years.

After about 14-18 months, the young males disperse and colonize into new areas. The female offspring tend to move "next door" in adjoining home ranges, as the females' ranges overlap. The male adolescent black bears, however, are sent away to avoid being killed by a mature male before the next breeding season begins.

Note the scars from the tree markings.

A final concept needs to be mentioned here before leaving black bear reproduction. Like armadillos (Issue 6) and river otters (Issue 8), female black bears also have the innate ability of *delayed implantation*. This development means that the sow can breed in June. A zygote (fertilized egg or ovum) can form but remain in a suspended, unattached state.

The female settles into the den when she is physically healthy and in good condition (has the proper body-to-fat ratio). Hormones enable the zygote to implant into the uterus lining.

During that June mating, she can become impregnated by two different boars. Therefore, they end up with cubs in the den who are half-related. Delayed implantation, therefore, can occur 5-6 months after breeding. If her body is not fit for pregnancy, then the zygotes will not

attach to her uterus and cease to develop.

Miscellaneous

A great deal has been learned about black bears by wildlife biologists from bear radio-tracking collars. Some of these devices operate using GPS or satellite. This tracking device enables bears to be located and observed in their habitat at various seasons.

As warm-blooded animals, bears can get rabies, but it is extremely rare. However, people can get a disease called

trichinosis from eating bear meat. This disease (known as trichinosis) is caused by a roundworm parasite found in the muscle tissue of bears, mountain lions, raccoons, grizzlies, wild pigs, and black bears. Eating undercooked meat leads to intense pain and, in severe cases, can affect vision. Proper cooking at the correct temperature and duration prevents infection.

Black bears seem well adapted to their environment but are a **keystone species**. They do benefit the ecosystem in that they are known for helping break down dead logs when searching for insects, bugs, and larvae. This practice helps break down the logs and enhances decay and its return to the soil. Bears are also known as seed dispersers. They eat a lot, so they poop ALOT (like all the time and huge big piles). The bear scat is not only full of seeds but provides excellent natural fertilizer for the seeds to germinate.

Their ability to eat just about anything almost ensures their survival. In addition, black bears have substantially strong legs that allow them to move or bend large objects like rocks, tree trunks, or limbs that get in their way and their food. The large, padded feet and strong, curved claws allow them the climb trees quickly to get to fruits, nuts, and honey (yes, black bears do love honey, but they are even fonder of the bee larvae). And, they have no reservations about invading bee farmers' hives. They love to eat bees and larvae inside a beehive, which is a good source of protein. Another adaptation is that of a long and sticky tongue. With such appetites and sharp claws, bears often hunt down and dig out of the ground wild yellow jacket nests.

The greatest threat to black bears is twofold: 1) too much exposure to people, 2) loss of habitat, territory division, changes in the environment due to global warming, and poaching. However, *bears are thriving nationwide*. There appears to be no bear population decline anywhere in the United States at this time.

Bears are best served and protected by the proper management and protection of large tracts of land, state and federal parks, Nature Conservatory lands, and state and national forests. The use of corridors (land set aside to connect other protected forests) ensures that bears continue to live and thrive in their chosen natural environment. Another means of conserving and protecting our bear population includes hunting and educating the public about bear attractants. Most bears don't have to have a large tract. They prefer it, but it's not a prerequisite.

What to do if you encounter a black bear

We have already seen how keen a bear's senses are. In all likelihood, you will never find yourself accidentally face-to-face with a black bear. The best policy is to remain alert and maintain a safe distance from bears. Canadian Rangers recommend keeping at least 100 yards away whenever possible. Generally, the only chance an average hiker will

stumble upon a bear up close and personal is when the wind is coming from the opposite direction, or the possibility of a bear totally focused and eating away in a blackberry patch. Such feasts greatly distract a bear's attention. They really will not want to leave and may wait until you are closer. It would be rare, but it could happen. Black bears' attacks on people are very infrequent, and most black bears can be easily scared away.

But, if you were to encounter a bear, remain calm and remember that the bear is likely more scared of you than you are of him. Remember, never run away from a bear, though that may be your first response to the adrenaline. A healthy bear can run 30 mph (48 kph). The fastest speed a human trained to run can travel only tops out at 28 mph (44.7 kph). *So, you are not going to outrun a bear!* Running could attract the bear and cause it to chase you. But be smart, and you can avoid that scenario.

First, stand and face the bear directly. Immediately stop and look and listen and see if you can determine if there are cubs present. *You do not want to be near the cubs with a mother bear present.* Don't antagonize a bear, but standing your ground sets precedence unless it is in your face. One key

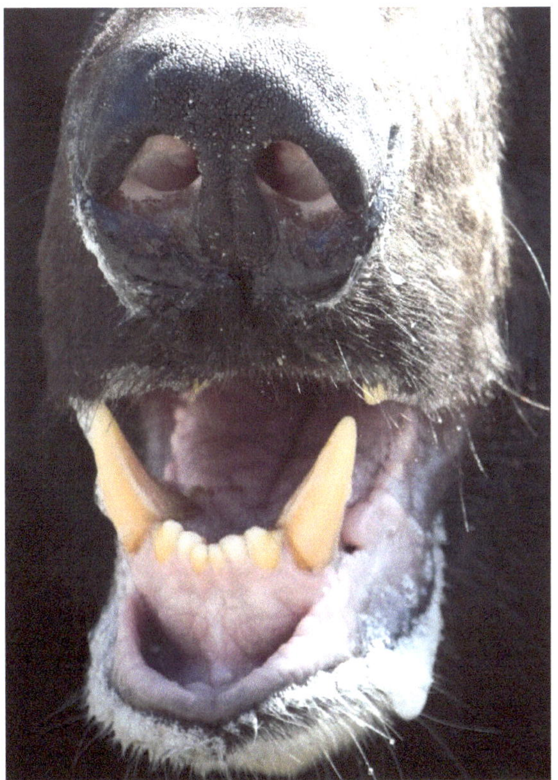

strategy is <u>not</u> to move fast but to make yourself appear larger than life. If you are wearing your backpack, leave it on as it makes you look larger.

Once you and the bear have made visual contact, and he or she appears not to want confrontation, then you will know your next move. In all likelihood, raising one's arms and tip-toeing will send the bear scurrying away. Making loud, gruff noises or banging something together loudly should send most black bears running for cover. Throwing rocks at bears scares most away. "Be large, be loud, and provide negative stimulus."[3] Also, some backpackers have suggested carrying air horns or bear repellant spray.[4]

A black bear that is feeling threatened does not roar or growl. Instead, it may slap the ground, huff loudly, or blow air forcefully through its nose or mouth. The bear may

To answer that age-old question: Does a bear poop in the woods?

snap, clack, or pop or chatter their teeth together loudly. Such behaviors are meant to scare the invader off. If a bear is still irritated and has not left the scene, then he or she may begin bluffing a charge. This conduct entails the bear running towards the person or animal and then veering

---

[3] Josh Wisdom, Missouri Wildlife Biologists.

[4] Those hiking in grizzly bear country often report that they carry bear repellant spray and an air horn. These items can scare off almost anything threat.

away. A bear that truly becomes aggressive towards a human will not make a sound but instead will stare, protrude its lower lip, and flatten its ears.

If the bear starts the quiet stand-down, you know a charge is about to occur. Don't wait for that.[5] Just keep in mind that an *ounce of prevention is indeed better than a pound of cure.* The best precaution is to stay alert and monitor the environment. Making noise on the trail is not bad unless you are engaged in wildlife photography or hunting. Typically, a bear will hear or smell a person long before they ever come into viewing distance, and then they are gone. Black bears, naturally, almost always seem to want to avoid confrontation.

Bear scat: usually filled with vegetation and insect parts in the spring and early summer. When berry season hits, scat is deposited as loose blobs that are filled with berries and seeds.

Most bear attacks are extremely rare (1 in 2.1 million chance), and the cases of aggression by black bears are even rarer. Fatal black bear attacks are so rare in the United States that they average about one per year. About one black bear in 1,000,000 ever attacks a

---

[5] One hiker found that before the bear reached the level of charging, he sprayed the bear repellant into the air and began retreating. Once the bear got wind of the repellant, it changed its mind and its direction ending the standoff.

human in a predatory manner.

Black bears are the titans of the forest. They have the rule. With their size, power, strength, and ability to eat almost anything, they are surviving very well in North America. If you see one, keep your distance. Get some good photographs, then move on. Remember, for the most part, you are in their home. Be a good guest. *Love life, love nature*

!

REVIEW

1. **What colors are black bears? What colors are rare?**

2. **To what size do black bears tend to grow?**

3. **Where does the mother black bears give birth to her newborn cubs?**

4. **What disease can one get from eating poorly cooked bear meat?**

5. **What should you do if you walk up on a black bear?**

BLACK BEAR

COLORING PAGE

http://www.supercoloring.com/coloring-pages/american-black-bear-family

Name:_______________________

Black Bears: Titans of the Forest

Carefully read each sentence and hint. Then record the answer in the appropriate squares.
Use the word bank, as needed.

Created using the Crossword Maker on TheTeachersCorner.net

urban   americanus   larvae   dead   smell   hungry   marking   require   die   implantation

fecal   bearclaws   confrontation   food   denning   curiosity

Across

3. What main factors determines whether bears sleep in a den?

5. The first job of the black bear after awakening from a winter sleep is to pass a _______ plub.

7. Bears, like armadillos and river otters, have the ability to delay __________.

8. Regarding habitat, bears prefer lot of foliage but they do not ______ it.

9. What is the species name given for the North American Black Bear?

10. Bears like honey, but what do they really love from a hive?

12. One habit bears do a lot of is ________ trees.

13. Black bears requiring the smallest range seem to be ______ bears.

14. Bears do not truly hibernate, instead what they do is called _______.

15. What can be said about a bear sows first cubs? Most of the _____.

Down

1. Two things drive a bear's attention: 1) food, ans 2) ________.

2. A bear's greatest sense is the sense of _______.

4. Bakeries have names a special donut-like dish after bears. What is this pastry called?

6. In most cases, encountering a black bear is safe because they want to avoid _______.

11. One thing we do know about bears is that they are always ________.

14. 'A fed bear is a ______ bear.'

INTERESTING SOURCES TO CONSIDER

12 amazing black bear facts: Discover Wildlife. Available at: https://www.discoverwildlife.com/animal-facts/mammals/facts-about-black-bears/

5 FACTS | North American Black Bear. Available at: https://youtu.be/hDiKSdfyVTo

American Black Bear. National Geographic. Available at: https://www.nationalgeographic.com/animals/mammals/a/american-black-bear/

American Black Bears. Encylopedia.com. Available at: . https://www.encyclopedia.com/people/history/historians-canadian-biographies/black-bear

Bear Wise: Meet the Black Bear. Available at: https://bearwise.org/all-about-black-bears/

Black Bears - National Park Animals for Kids. Available at: https://youtu.be/QaRGgipzehU

Black Bears. Available at: https://defenders.org/wildlife/black-bear

Black Bears. The National Wildlife Federation. Available at: https://www.nwf.org/Educational-Resources/Wildlife-Guide/Mammals/Black-Bear

Interesting Facts about Black Bears. Available at: https://www.visitbigsky.com/blog/interesting-facts-about-black-bears-1/

Love of Nature Series. APE-Learning. Available online at: http://amazon.com/author/richardnesmith

Quick Black Bear Facts. North American Bear Center. Available at: https://bear.org/quick-black-bear-facts/

The American Black Bear: Everything You Need To Know!. Available at: https://youtu.be/fsg5vjwchLs

The Bear Whisperer: They're Huge And Hungry! The Bears Are Back In Town! | Real Wild Documentary. Available at: https://youtu.be/WJDQkZH10uo

ABOUT THE AUTHOR

Richard NeSmith is a native of Florida, USA. He grew up wading through the swamps of central Florida with his two younger brothers during the pre-Disney era and unknowingly, falling in love with biology, wildlife, and nature. He has lived in seven American states, twice in Australia and once in Mexico City. He holds eight university degrees and has taught for 14 years in secondary schools, here and abroad, and another 13 years as a professor in several American universities. His service includes professor of science education, Dean of Education, Campus Dean, as well as an online instructor. His passion for learning (and *how we learn*) did not develop until *after* graduating from high school. His only explanation for this is that *having a goal made all the difference in the world*. He enjoys reading, hiking, nature photography, golf, and tennis.

http://richardnesmith.obior.cc

Applied Principles of Education & Learning *presents*

APE-Learning

AMAZON AUTHOR's PAGE:

https://www.amazon.com/author/richardnesmith

Educational, wildlife, and naturalist books available by Dr. Richard NeSmith.

Issue 1
Raccoons:
Friendly Bandits
Dr. Richard NeSmith

Issue 2
Sandhill Cranes
&
Pileated Woodpeckers
Flaming Redheads
Dr. Richard NeSmith

Issue 3
American
Alligators
&
Crocodiles
Dr. Richard NeSmith

Issue 4
Bobcats:
Ghostly Elusive
Dr. Richard NeSmith

Issue 5
Foxes:
Sneaky Rascals
Dr. Richard NeSmith

Issue 6
Armadillo:
Little Armored One
Dr. Richard NeSmith

http://amazon.com/author/richardnesmith

[i] Special thanks to the following who kindly provided permission to use their photographs.

From Unsplash: Simon Infanger, TheOtherKev, Ben Owen, JT-ray-spyu, Yann Allegre, Pete Nuij, Vincent Van Zalinge, Sung Jin Cho, noaa,

From Pixabay: Brigachtal, Evelyn Villing, Skeeze, Art Tower, David Cardinez, Paul Brennan, Sébastien Rys, Alex Sutcliffe, and Wahle

Special thanks to likeminded friends who love wildlife and who willingly shared their wonderful photos: *Mr. Phil Stone, Josh Putnam, Peyton Maddox, Stacey Diamond,* and *Eric Berg*.

In addition, my *special thanks* to **Josh Wisdom**, Missouri Wildlife biologists, for his insights and stories, which were very inspirational and informative.

Thank you all.